Love to Dance

Ballet

Angela Royston

Heinemann
LIBRARY
Chicago, Illinois

© 2013 Raintree
an imprint of Capstone Global Library, LLC
Chicago, Illinois

Edited by Nancy Dickmann, Catherine Veitch, and Abby Colich
Designed by Cynthia Della-Rovere
Picture research by Elizabeth Alexander
Production by Alison Parsons
Originated by Capstone Global Library Ltd
Printed and bound in China by CTPS

16 15 14 13 12
10 9 8 7 6 5 4 3 2 1

Library of Congress Cataloging-in-Publication Data
Royston, Angela, 1945-
    Ballet / Angela Royston.—1st ed.
      p. cm.—(Love to dance)
Includes bibliographical references and index.
 ISBN 978-1-4109-4920-2 (hb)—ISBN 978-1-4109-4925-7 (pb) 1. Ballet—Juvenile literature. I. Title.
    GV1787.5.R69 2013
    792.8—dc23   2012019128

Acknowledgments
We would like to thank the following for permission to reproduce photographs: Alamy pp. 9 (© Pictorial Press Ltd), 13 (© Lebrecht Music and Arts Photo Library), 14 (© Patrick Baldwin), 16 (© Bubbles Photolibrary), 18 (© Patrick Baldwin), 29 (© van hilversum); Corbis pp. 7 (© Paul Cunningham), 24 (© John Bryson/ Sygma), 26 (© Robbie Jack); Getty Images pp. 6 (APIC), 8 (Ian Gavan), 15 (Gjon Mili/Time Life Pictures), 19 (Gjon Mili/Time Life Pictures), 27 (Ian Gavan); Rex Features pp. 12, 25 (Alastair Muir); Shutterstock pp. title page (© Dmitry Yashkin), 4-5 (© Jack.Q), 10 (© Igor Bulgarin), 11 (© Jack.Q), 20, 21 (© s74), 23 (© Dmitry Yashkin); SuperStock pp. 17 (© Image Source), 22 (© Fancy Collection), 28 (© Flirt).

Design features reproduced with permission of Shutterstock (© AZ, © Christopher Elwell, © Arkady Mazor, © Studio DMM Photography, Designs & Art, © Plus69, © Studio DMM Photography, Designs & Art, © Robert Young).

Cover photograph of English National Ballet's production of *Swan Lake* reproduced with permission of Corbis (© Paul Cunningham).

We would like to thank Annie Beserra for her invaluable help in the preparation of this book.

Contents

Some words are shown in bold, **like this**. You can find out what they mean by looking in the glossary.

This Is Ballet!

Two dancers move gracefully across the stage. The music swells and the other dancers whirl lightly around them. The audience does not make a sound.

Why I dance

Saskia Beskow, a dancer with the New York City Ballet, says, "It is natural for me to move to music. It makes me so happy to dance."

How Ballet Began

Ballet was popular in the royal palaces in Italy and France. King Louis the Fourteenth of France adored ballet and loved to dance. He even danced as Apollo, the Greek god of the sun.

King Louis was known as the "Sun King."

Pantomime

Ballet dancers have always used special gestures, or movements, called **pantomime**, to help tell a story.

Classical Ballet

Many classical ballets were created in St. Petersburg, in Russia, after 1850. The ballets included *The Nutcracker, Swan Lake,* and *Sleeping Beauty.* These ballets told a story, like a fairy tale.

A scene from
The Nutcracker

Dying swan

Russian ballerina Anna Pavlova is most famous for dancing "The Dying Swan." When Pavlova was dying she asked to hold her swan costume.

Basic Move: The Arabesque

An **arabesque** is a common position in ballet. The dancer stands tall and stretches out one leg behind. The arms are stretched out gracefully.

The move is called *arabesque en l'air* when the leg behind is lifted.

Here the male partner supports the female in an *arabesque en l'air.*

French terms

The first ballet school began in 1669 in Paris, France. Most ballet steps and positions still have French names today.

Changing Styles

About 100 years ago, ballet companies in Paris, New York, and London began to dance new, shorter ballets. The dancing was more important than the story in these new ballets.

Spectacular sight

Sometimes famous artistic people like Pablo Picasso and Coco Chanel made the sets and the costumes.

Skills

Ballet dancers must be athletic as well as elegant. They need to be flexible and have strong muscles to perform different moves.

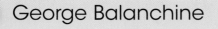

George Balanchine

Choreographer

A **choreographer** creates all the steps in a ballet. George Balanchine is a famous choreographer. He started the New York City Ballet. Balanchine created more than 400 ballets in his lifetime.

Practice, Practice, Practice

Professional dancers practice every day. First, they warm up at the barre, which is a long wooden pole fixed along a wall. They might do **_pliés_**. They stand tall with their legs turned out and bend their knees over their toes.

barre

Dancers follow the actions of their teacher.

The ballet dancers then move away from the barre. They move on to center work. They practice jumps, turns, and balances.

Tricky Move: The Big Jump

Grand jeté means "big jump." It is a **dynamic** way to cross the stage. The dancer does the splits as he or she jumps through the air, with arms stretched out.

Jumping and turning

In the **double tour en l'air**, the dancer jumps into the air and turns around twice. It is much harder than it looks!

What to Wear

Most dancers wear a leotard when they practice. Leotards are comfortable and stretch as they move. Dancers perform in specially designed costumes. In a classical ballet, the ballerinas usually wear tutus.

tutu

Ballet shoes

Ballet shoes are the most important part of a dancer's clothes. They are soft, to allow feet to arch and stretch.

En Pointe

Professional ballerinas often dance on the tips of their toes. This is called **en pointe**. Ballerinas wear special *pointe* shoes that support their feet. The shoes have hard ends and flat toes.

Be patient!

Your ballet teacher will advise you when you are ready to go *en pointe*. If you start too young, it can hurt your feet.

Tricky Move: Fish Dive

A **pas de deux** means "a step for two" in French. It is a dance for two dancers, usually a man and a woman. It uses jumps and lifts. It sometimes ends with a spectacular fish dive.

Rudolf Nureyev and Margot Fonteyn

The fish dive

The ballerina leaps into the arms of the male dancer, who swoops her down and forward, arching like a fish.

The Performance

You can watch ballet on television and on DVDs. But the most exciting way to see it is in the theater. A large number of people are needed to put on a ballet.

The Nutcracker

Backstage

Set designers and costume designers work for months to make the sets and costumes. The dancers practice and rehearse lots of times.

Give It a Try!

Ballet is a lot of fun and great exercise, but you should learn it with a trained teacher. Ballet makes your body stronger, and it helps you to balance. Joining a class is also a good way to make new friends.

Getting confident

Ballet makes you more confident about your body. When you are ready, you can perform for your family and friends.

Glossary

arabesque position with one leg stretched behind and one or both arms reaching forward

choreographer person who creates and designs the steps of a dance

double tour en l'air French for "a double turn in the air." It is a jump in which the dancer turns twice in the air.

dynamic describes something that is energetic and exciting

en pointe French for "on point." It is when a ballerina balances and dances on the tips of her toes.

grand jeté French for "big jump." It is a jump in which the dancer does the splits in mid-air.

pantomime way of telling a story or showing thoughts and feelings using hand or head movements

pas de deux French for "step for two." It is a dance for two people.

plié French for "bend." It is a movement in which dancers bend their knees over their toes and then stretch their legs straight again.

professional person who is paid for doing a job

set designer person who decides what the stage in a ballet will look like. This includes objects—for example, trees or tables—and painted background panels showing a scene.

Find Out More

Books

Bussell, Darcey. *The Ballet Book*. New York:
    Dorling Kindersley, 2006.

Dillman, Lisa. *Ballet* (Get Going!: Hobbies).
    Chicago: Heinemann Library, 2006.

Graves, Karen M. *Ballet Dance* (Snap Books).
    Mankato, Minn.: Capstone, 2008.

Hackett, Jane. *Ballet: A Step-by-Step Guide to the Secrets
    of Ballet* (How To). New York: Dorling Kindersley, 2011.

Websites

Facthound offers a safe, fun way to find Internet sites related
to this book. All of the sites on Facthound have been
researched by our staff.

Here's all you do:
Visit www.facthound.com

Type in this code: 9781410949202

Index